WHAT DOES THE VICE PRESIDENT DO?

**We the People:
U.S. Government at Work**

Kevin Winn

Published in the United States of America by:

CHERRY LAKE PRESS
2395 South Huron Parkway, Suite 200, Ann Arbor, Michigan 48104
www.cherrylakepress.com

Reading Adviser: Beth Walker Gambro, MS, Ed., Reading Consultant, Yorkville, IL
Content Adviser: Mark Richards, Ph.D., Professor, Dept. of Political Science, Grand Valley State University, Allendale, MI

Photo Credits: cover: Maverick Pictures/Shutterstock; page 5: Adam Schultz/The White House; page 6: Corcoran Collection/
National Gallery of Art; page 7: Princeton University, gift of William Otis Morse, Class of 1902; page 8: Army Sgt. Charlotte Carulli/
U.S. Department of Defense; page 9: National Portrait Gallery, Smithsonian Institution (top), Barack Obama/Flickr (bottom);
page 11: Abbie Rowe/National Park Service/Harry S. Truman Library & Museum; page 12: Gerald R. Ford Presidential Foundation;
page 14: Alex Fox Echols III/U.S. Air Force; page 16: © Frederic Legrand – COMEO/Shutterstock; page 19: © Michael F. Hiatt/
Shutterstock; page 20: © Mangkorn Danggura/Shutterstock; page 21: © Janet Julie Vanatko/Shutterstock

Cherry Lake Press is an imprint of Cherry Lake Publishing Group.

Library of Congress Cataloging-in-Publication Data

Names: Winn, Kevin P., author.
Title: What does the vice president do? / Kevin Winn.
Description: Ann Arbor, Michigan : Cherry Lake Publishing, [2023] | Series: We the people: U.S. government at work | Audience: Grades 2-3
Summary: "Young readers will discover what the U.S. vice president does and learn about the basic building blocks of the United States
    of America. They'll also learn about how they play a key role in American democracy. Series is aligned to 21st Century Skills curriculum
    standards. Engaging inquiry-based sidebars encourage students to Think, Create, Guess, and Ask Questions. Includes table of contents,
    glossary, index, author biography, and sidebars"– Provided by publisher.
Identifiers: LCCN 2022039927 | ISBN 9781668919422 (hardcover) | ISBN 9781668920442 (paperback) | ISBN 9781668921777 (ebook) |
    ISBN 9781668923108 (pdf)
Subjects: LCSH: Vice presidents–United States–Juvenile literature. | Executive power–United States–Juvenile literature. | United States–
    Politics and government–Juvenile literature.
Classification: LCC JK609.5 .W57 2023 | DDC 352.23/90973–dc23/eng/20220915
LC record available at https://lccn.loc.gov/2022039927

Cherry Lake Press would like to acknowledge the work of the Partnership for 21st Century Learning, a Network of Battelle for Kids. Please
visit http://www.battelleforkids.org/networks/p21 for more information.

Printed in the United States of America
Corporate Graphics

CONTENTS

THE HISTORY OF THE U.S. VICE PRESIDENT

The Vice President of the United States has an important job. They're the second most powerful person in the **executive branch**. While the president has the most power, the vice president must be ready to become president in case something happens to the president.

Kamala Harris is the first woman to be vice president of the United States.

The process of electing a vice president has changed. Originally, the vice president was the person who ran for president but came in second place. For example, Thomas Jefferson was elected president in 1800.

President Thomas Jefferson (left) and Vice President Aaron Burr (right) did not get along.

Make a Guess!

After serving as vice president, six people have been elected president. Why do you think they were successful? Why might others have been unsuccessful?

Aaron Burr came in second. He became the vice president. Unfortunately, the two men didn't get along. The process needed to change.

In 1804, the process switched. Instead, a person who ran for president chose a running mate. This means that the president and vice president run together. When Americans vote, they vote for both the president and vice president at the same time.

President Joe Biden was former President Barack Obama's Vice President.

Just like the president, there are some requirements to becoming vice president. This person must be:

- A **natural-born citizen**
- At least 35 years old
- A continuous U.S. resident for at least the last 14 years

John Adams was the first vice president. He then became the second president.

THE VICE PRESIDENT'S DUTIES

Vice presidents don't have the power that the president has. But they still have important duties.

Vice presidents have become president after presidents have died in or **resigned** from office. John Tyler was the first vice president to take over for a president. President William Henry Harrison died after only 31 days in office!

Vice President Harry Truman was sworn in as president two hours after President Franklin D. Roosevelt died in office.

Vice President Gerald Ford was sworn in as president after President Richard Nixon resigned.

The vice president may take on presidential duties at other times too. The Twenty-fifth Amendment to the U.S. Constitution gives vice presidents presidential power for different reasons. These include times when presidents are hospitalized or having surgery.

The vice president **presides** over the U.S. Senate. The U.S. Senate is part of Congress. When the senators vote on a **bill** and are equally split, the vice president votes. The vice president acts as tiebreaker during these times. The vice president can vote to either pass or fail the bill.

While vice presidents don't have many official duties, they do assist the president. They help advise the president. They represent the president at some events. They also **certify** presidential elections.

Ask Questions!

Sometimes Americans don't think the vice president is very important. But the vice president can help pass laws in Congress. Why should voters think about this? Why does it matter?

Vice President Mike Pence met leaders from around the world.

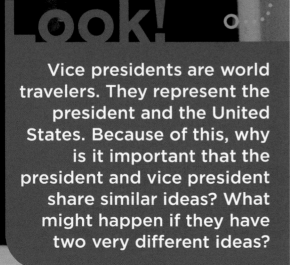

Look!

Vice presidents are world travelers. They represent the president and the United States. Because of this, why is it important that the president and vice president share similar ideas? What might happen if they have two very different ideas?

Sometimes vice presidents travel to different countries. They meet with world leaders. The president can't be everywhere at once, so the vice president represents the United States.

The vice president travels all over the world to meet foreign leaders. Air traffic control calls any U.S. Air Force plane carrying the vice president "Air Force Two".

Former Vice President Al Gore has spoken out about climate change since he was in office in the 1990s.

THE VICE PRESIDENCY TODAY

The vice presidency has become a more powerful position in recent years. The vice president often takes on the president's **agenda**. When they have a strong partnership, they act as a team.

In recent years, vice presidents have had a lot of knowledge about certain topics. For example, Vice President Al Gore helped with President Bill Clinton's focus on the environment. Vice President Dick Cheney assisted President George W. Bush with military issues.

There aren't many requirements to become vice president. Yet most people who have held the position have been White men. This changed in 2020. Kamala Harris became the first woman and person of color to hold the position.

Think!

It wasn't until 2020 that a woman became vice president. Kamala Harris was the first. Why do you think this is? What barriers has she helped break down? What other women do you think should run for vice president? Why?

Vice President Kamala Harris is the first woman, first Black, and first South Asian American vice president.

ACTIVITY

Write it out! You've learned that the vice president is elected. That means it's important that they listen to the people they serve. Write a letter to the vice president about something that matters to you. Make sure to include your address so they can write back!

GLOSSARY

agenda (uh-JEN-duh) plan for moving ideas forward

amendment (uh-MEND-muhnt) change or addition to the U.S. Constitution

bill (BIL) draft of a law

certify (SUHR-tuh-fye) make official

executive branch (ek-ZEH-kyoo-tiv BRANCH) part of government that includes the president, vice president, and the president's cabinet

natural-born citizen (NAH-chuh-ruhl SIH-tuh-zuhn) someone born within the United States, its territories, or districts

presides (prih-ZYDZ) is in charge of

resigned (rih-ZYND) quit a job or position

FIND OUT MORE

Books

Baxter, Roberta. *The Creation of the U.S. Constitution.* Ann Arbor, MI: Cherry Lake Publishing, 2014.

Bedesky, Baron. *What Is a Government?* New York, NY: Crabtree Publishing Co., 2008.

Cheney, Lynne. *We the People.* New York, NY: Simon & Schuster, 2012.

Christelow, Eileen. *Vote!* New York, NY: Clarion Books, 2018.

McDivitt, Lindsey. *Truth and Honor: The President Ford Story.* Ann Arbor, MI: Sleeping Bear Press, 2020.

Websites

Ben's Guide to the U.S. Government
https://bensguide.gpo.gov
Let Ben Franklin guide you through the whos and whats of our government.

iCivics
https://icivics.org
Find out how you can be an informed and involved citizen.

INDEX

ABOUT THE AUTHOR

Kevin Winn is a children's book writer and researcher. He focuses on issues of racial justice and educational equity in his work. In 2020, Kevin earned his doctorate in Educational Policy and Evaluation from Arizona State University.